My Brother Charlie

written by

HOLLY ROBINSON PEETE

and

RYAN ELIZABETH PEETE

with

Denene Millner

pictures by
SHANE W. EVANS

Scholastic Press
New York

We've always been together—even in Mommy's tummy—my twin brother, Charlie, and me.

We still share lots
of things:

Curly hair and brown eyes.

How much we love hot chocolate
with marshmallows.

Our dog, Harriett.

Rolling in the grass.

Music.

Football.

And names that start

with the letter C—Callie and Charlie.

But being twins doesn't make us exactly the same.

I'm two minutes younger than Charlie.

I can stare for hours at the Big Dipper and the moon.

And I love to *talk*.

Charlie is skinnier and goofier than me.

He hates math.

When he looks at the sky, he finds jets and helicopters.

And sometimes my brother gets very quiet.

BiG Yellow Book

Math for Kids

The 1 plus 1 book

animal facts

When we were babies, I pointed out flowers and cats and fireflies.

I snuggled and giggled with Mommy on dark nights.

And told Mommy again and again how much I love her.

But Charlie was different. He wouldn't play with me.

Or kiss Mommy's cheeks when she hugged him.

And he didn't say "I love you." Seems those words were locked deep inside my brother.

Everyone told Mommy not to worry.

"He's just being a boy," they said.

But Mommy knew there was something different about Charlie.

I knew it, too.

As we grew older, Mommy watched Charlie very carefully. She and I could see he was struggling. Then Mommy discovered that Charlie's brain works in a special way, because Charlie has autism.

It's harder for Charlie to make friends. Or show his feelings. Or stay safe.

One doctor even told Mommy that Charlie would never say "I love you."

That made Mommy and me saddest of all.

I have learned from Charlie that love doesn't always come from what you say. It can also come from what you *do*. And so we do right by Charlie. We love Charlie strong. We watch over him with the might of angels. We have to.

Children's Doctor

When Charlie wants something, nothing stops him. Even when it's dangerous. And there are days when it's hard to be Charlie's sister. Sometimes he can ruin the best playdates. Other times he seems so far away, like when he won't look at me. Or speak. Or play.

I wish I could crawl inside Charlie's world to move things around for him and for me. I know Charlie wants to be in my world, fitting in, making friends, having fun, and laughing.

There are good times with Charlie, too—when Charlie looks right at me and welcomes me with his smile. He lets me touch his face.

He laughs when we lock fingers in a holding-hands game. That's Charlie's

I love you, said in the silly ways we play together.

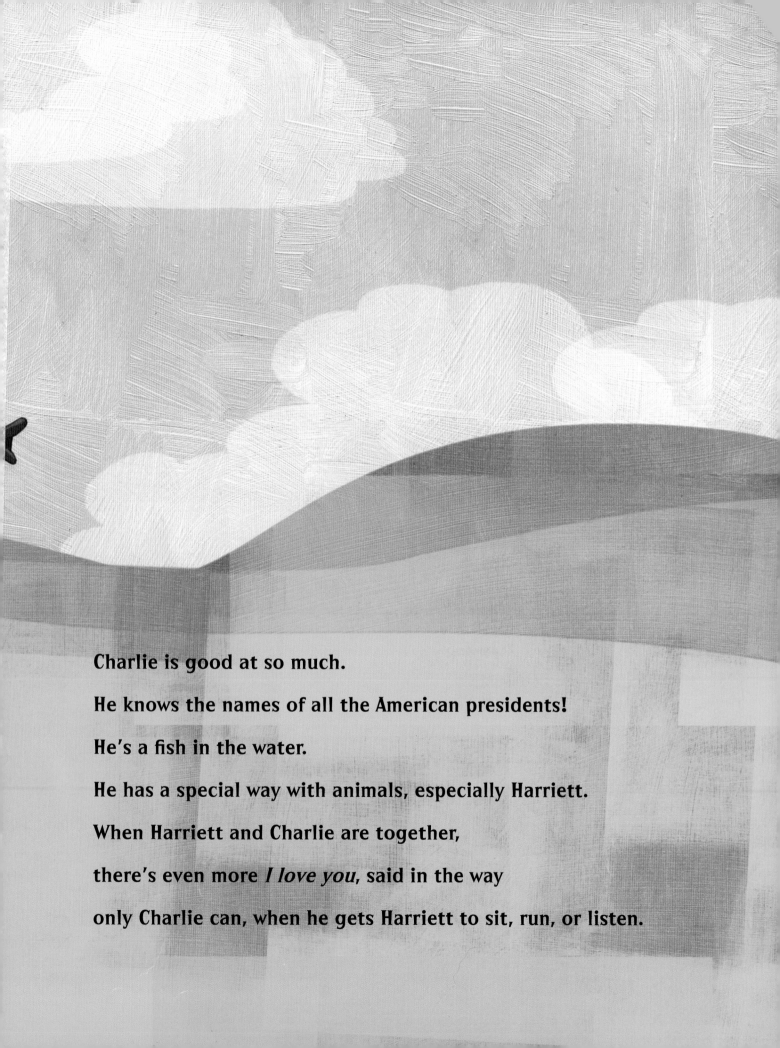

Charlie is good at so much.

He knows the names of all the American presidents!

He's a fish in the water.

He has a special way with animals, especially Harriett.

When Harriett and Charlie are together,

there's even more *I love you*, said in the way

only Charlie can, when he gets Harriett to sit, run, or listen.

Charlie's got a mind that tests things.

Shoelaces.

Paper clips.

Apples.

Pinecones.

And he enjoys sharing.

He likes to show off his shell collection, his new sneakers, and how well he plays "Itsy Bitsy Spider" on the piano.

Charlie likes to share how sweet he is and how much he cares about other people. When I fall off my bike or bump my head, Charlie comes running. He always makes my hurts feel better with the caring that comes from his eyes.

Sometimes, when Charlie can find the words—when they unlock themselves from inside him—he *does* say "I love you."

I will always remember the first time I heard
him say it. So clear and kind. So Charlie.

I banged my toe hard, and cried.
There was my brother, patting my back,
saying over and over again,
"Don't cry, Callie, I love you."

It wasn't just the words that were so strong.

It was the love that Charlie showed me, just by being there.

"I love you, too, Charlie," came from me fast.

Charlie has autism. But autism doesn't have Charlie.

If you ever get to meet my brother, you'll feel lucky to be his friend.

He won't care if you have the coolest sneakers, or if you are the best

at sports. He'll just like you for who you really are. That's Charlie.

I'm blessed to be Charlie's sister and to share so much. I count my "Charlie Blessings" every day. At the very top of my "Charlie Blessings" list is the love Charlie and I have for each other.

Said in so
many ways.

ACKNOWLEDGMENTS

Thanks to the entire Robinson and Peete families for the village of support for this project. Ryan, I am so proud of the daughter and sister you are and the writer you are becoming. Robinson and Roman, you are terrific sons and supportive, loving brothers. Rodney, you are the best partner I could have chosen for this journey. Mom and Matt, thank you for consistent nonjudgmental support. I love you so much.

Andrea Davis Pinkney, you have been a tremendous editor, but more important, I have found you to be a genuine and intriguing ally. I have learned so much from you! Jason and Jennifer, thanks for getting my back in this process! Denene Millner, thank you for your invaluable editorial support and guidance. Love to uber-talented Shane Evans.

Special thanks also to Jason McElwain, Al Roker, Magic Johnson, Marion Wright Edelman, Dan Marino, Oprah Winfrey, *Essence* magazine, *People* magazine, Suzanne and Bob Wright, and my friends at Target Foundation/Corporation.

Finally: To my RJ. Thank you for teaching Mommy how to slow down and count her "RJ Blessings." I cherish everything about you. I am so proud of the young man you are. Thank you for understanding that sharing your story is selfless and crucial to helping other kids. You are my hero. —HRP

Thanks to my brothers, RJ, Robinson, and Roman, and to my dad, Rodney. Mommy, it was an amazing experience working with you. I love you so much. —REP

LIBRARY OF CONGRESS CATALOGING-IN-PUBLICATION DATA

Peete, Holly Robinson, 1964-
My brother Charlie : a sister's story of autism / by Holly Robinson Peete and Ryan Elizabeth Peete ;
illustrated by Shane W. Evans. — 1st ed.   p. cm.
Summary: A girl tells what it is like living with her twin brother who has autism and sometimes finds it hard to communicate with words, but who, in most ways, is just like any other boy. Includes author's note about autism.
ISBN-13: 978-0-545-09466-5
1. Children's writings, American. [1. Autism—Fiction. 2. Twins—Fiction. 3. Brothers and sisters—Fiction.]
I. Peete, Ryan. II. Evans, Shane, ill. III. Title.   PZ7.P3567My 2010   [E]—dc22   2009005589

10 9 8 7 6 5   16 17 18

Printed in Malaysia 108 • First edition, March 2010

The text type in this book was set in Sproket BT. The display type in this book was set in F 2 F Mad Zine Whip.
The art in this book was created using mixed mediums. Book design by Marijka Kostiw

Holly Robinson Peete and Ryan Elizabeth Peete have arranged for five percent of their royalty earnings for this book to go to the HollyRod4Kids Foundation to help children with autism gain access to affordable treatments and therapies. The purchase of the book is not tax deductible. HollyRod4Kids may be contacted at: HollyRod Foundation, 9250 Wilshire Blvd., Suite LL15, Beverly Hills, CA 90212 (www.hollyrod.com).

This book is dedicated to all the families to whom autism has brought challenges, heartache, and triumphs. I wish you profound patience, deep breaths, and strength during your journey. Our children are unique angels. —HRP

I dedicate this book to other kids who have brothers and sisters with autism. I hope you will embrace your siblings and help them be more successful in life. —REP

Thank you, God. This book is dedicated to all of the children of Lesotho, Africa. Continue to dream and inspire your country. Also, to my new-found family in Botswana and South Africa—be blessed. —Your brother "Tshegofatso" (SWE)

WHY WE WROTE THIS BOOK—AND HOW IT CAN HELP YOU

We offer this book as a gift to families struggling with autism and to those who have no autism in their immediate families but who have friends facing it. *My Brother Charlie* is a book about how special all children are, and how every one of us can find value in the uniqueness of people.

HOLLY ROBINSON PEETE

My oldest son, RJ, was born two minutes before his twin sister, Ryan. Both newborns were beautiful, and like every mother, when they arrived, I was filled with a joy that is beyond description. RJ and Ryan were very talkative toddlers. I will always remember this because one day, RJ's chattiness stopped, almost suddenly. I noticed, too, that while Ryan continued to pass several developmental milestones, RJ ceased making eye contact and wouldn't answer me when I called him.

In 2000, when RJ was three, we got the diagnosis of autism. Autism is defined by the medical community as a neurobiological disorder. According to Autism Speaks, a national autism advocacy organization, 1 in 150 individuals is diagnosed with autism. I felt a profound sense of hopelessness, confusion, and anger. My husband, Rodney, and I refer to that as the "never" day, since we were told by a doctor that RJ would *never* accomplish many things. The two *nevers* that were the most painful were that he would *never* verbally connect with us in a spontaneous fashion and would *never* say he loved us without being prompted.

Today, with the help of many caring professionals, our boy has checked these *nevers* and many others off his list. Like most parents, my husband and I continue to do everything we can to aid RJ's progress. Although we still face many challenges, he continues to delight us with his smarts, humor, athleticism, and charm.

RYAN ELIZABETH PEETE

I love my twin brother. He is extraordinary even if he can be annoying.

My goal with this book is to let kids and their parents in on a little secret: Kids with autism are valuable human beings with real feelings, even though they can't always express them. I feel it is up to those of us who don't have autism to change ourselves so that we can better understand people who have it.

At school, if you think someone is weird just because he can't express himself, he might have autism. Please don't tease that person; instead, go and play with him. My twin brother, RJ, was not so popular at the beginning of fourth grade. He said, "If I could tell people one thing about autism it would be that I don't want to be this way." That's when I put together a program for my class called Autism 101.

This important lesson helped my friends and their parents become more accepting of me and my family. Here are the ideas we have found most helpful.

> If someone who has autism doesn't respond right away when you speak to him, it doesn't mean he's being rude. Socializing can be challenging for people with autism.

> Many people have trouble making friends, but it's even harder for boys and girls with autism. Include people with autism even more than you would others.

> We are all special in our own way. Focus on what kids do well. Ask others about their strengths and acknowledge that everyone has strengths *and* weaknesses.

> People with autism are exceptionally smart, but their brains are wired differently. It can take them longer to process information. Please be patient.